25 DIRECT MAIL SUCCESS SECRETS THAT CAN MAKE YOU RICH!

By T.J. Rohleder
(A.K.A. America's "Blue Jeans Millionaire")
Founder of the Direct-Response Network

Also by T.J. Rohleder:

The Black Book of Marketing Secrets (Series)
The Ultimate Wealth-Maker
Ruthless Marketing Attack
How to Start Your Own Million Dollar Business
Five Secrets That Will Triple Your Profits
24 Simple and Easy Ways to Get Rich Quick
Secrets of the Blue Jeans Millionaire
Shortcut Secrets to Creating High-Profit Products
Fast Track to Riches
Four Magical Secrets to Building a Fabulous Fortune
How to Create a Hot Selling Internet Product in One Day

Introduction

Hey there! This is T.J. Rohleder of the Direct Response Network and M.O.R.E. Inc. and I've got an exciting publication here for you to study. In its pages, I reveal 25 Direct Mail Success Secrets that can make you as rich as you want to be. How do I know that they work? Well, my company's been using them for 20 years and so far we've made over $110 million in our various endeavors. Not all of that money was earned through direct mail, but the great majority of it was. And though I'm proud of that, I'm not trying to brag here; I'm just trying to show you how utterly effective, and profitable, these secrets can be. I'll be presenting them in two main sections. Part I will cover what you need to do, while Part II will cover the specifics on *how* to do it.

Direct mail is the one thing that's has made us more money than anything we've ever done. When my wife and I first started our business, we advertised in magazines like most mail order companies do. But we quickly switched to direct mail instead. We have this graph of when we first started our business that shows our monthly sales figures. In the first six months we were just doing space advertising, and yes, there's a nice, steady rise. When we started doing direct mail, though, the curve shot straight up like a giant mountain. While we were doing well in the beginning, direct mail is what made us millions of dollars. That's why it's so exciting to be able to pass along this information.

Back when we ran our ads in a national magazine, we had the potential of reaching millions of people. Sure, that *sounds* great, but here's the reality -- how many people do you know who do more than glance at most advertisements? Not many. Then there's the competition you face -- you have to stand out or your ad will get lost in a sea of others like it. But when you take advantage of direct mail, you know your letter will go directly to your target a good 99% of the time. You don't know for sure whether they'll look at it or not, but you're definitely more targeted -- that is, you have more control over whether or not someone sees your advertisement. You'll put it right in their hands. They can read it if they want to, or they can trash it. The big thrill is that if only a small percentage of your market reads and responds to your ad, you can still make a profit, too.

I believe that the best form of marketing, even after a century of use, is *still* direct mail -- a sentiment that at least 80% of the real pros in direct response marketing will agree with. Even in the face of print ads, TV ads, radio, and the Internet, there's no question about it. If you learn how to do direct mail properly, you're a mile ahead of the pack. In fact, you're a *thousand* miles ahead of the pack. The best news is that anyone who has their own retail businesses can use direct mail to boost their profits.

I'm enthusiastic about direct mail for three main reasons. Number One, there are millions of people that you can mail your offer to. Number Two, you can reach these people for relatively small amounts of money. Number Three, you can get a super-fast return on your investment. For example: in one seven-week period a few years back, we brought in $400,000 on one direct mail campaign. Another time, a couple of years before that, we brought in over *$2.5 million* in just six months time on a direct mail campaign. Obviously, this is a lot of money, very, *very* quickly. Again, I'm not presenting these figures to brag -- I just want you to know the amazing potential of direct mail.

In this publication I'll be covering twenty-five of our secrets -- but within each of these topics are many more ideas that I'll explore. I truly believe you're going to find hundreds of ideas here that can help you start making money *immediately* with direct mail. So let's jump in with both feet, shall we?

Part I: What to Do

Let's start out with definition of direct mail: that's **Secret Number One**. A lot of people are unclear about what Direct Mail is. In fact, it can be so many things. Primarily, direct mail is a way of targeting a market by mailing out offers, thereby reaching customers and prospects by means of their physical mailboxes in a personal, one-to-one fashion. You might mail 100,000 pieces of direct mail -- sales letters, postcards, self-mailers, or almost anything else that you can put in the mail -- but you nevertheless aim your offer at one person. You should talk directly to that person in your material; that's what makes it immediate, one-to-one.

We use direct mail for two things in our business. One is for attracting new customers; another is to get more business from the customers we already have. This is a simple strategy that takes one thing into account: the fact that marketing is all of the things that you do to attract new customers to your business. Then you simply resell those customers, over and over again, by creating additional products or services for them to buy. Direct mail is the best way that we've ever found to be able to go back to our customers repeatedly.

Attracting new customers is the lifeblood of any business. This is **Secret Number Two**. Now, admittedly, the profits on new customers will be very small compared to the profits you get when contacting and mailing your regular customers. The new customer generally comes in at a slight profit or sometimes at a break-even point -- and sometimes even at a small loss. The big profit comes on the back end, where you consistently work your customer list and sell them new products and services.

When you're dealing with new customers, you have to keep one thing in mind: they don't know you and they don't know your company. So you've got that hurdle to get over. Your repeat customers *do* know you. They know you're reliable and they know what kinds of products you send out, so old customers are always the best way to test new products. The way to get the *new* customers is to make a sensational offer, even if you don't make much of a profit (if any). It's done just to bring them into the fold. So when it comes to attracting new customers, people you've never done business with, there are certain things that you have to do that are different.

One of the ways we've effectively drawn new people in is by putting together initial offers that make it very easy for people to respond. We've developed all kinds of low-end offers for new customers. We offer them something for free or for a low cost, which makes it easy to make that first sale. Then we start building the relationship. You please them by sending them a package that they get excited about. They say, "Boy, this company sent it to me quickly, and what they send me was every bit as good as or better than what they said they would send!" Once you've brought them in that way, they have the great possibility of becoming long-term customers.

Secret Number Three is getting more business from your current customers. I think it's extremely important for you to understand something that someone told me when we first got started. This was just an analogy, but it really sank in for us: they told us that attracting new customers is like pedaling a bicycle uphill, whereas doing more business with the customers you have is like coasting that same bike downhill. I've thought about that quote many times since I heard it, because it's the gospel truth. It's much easier to do more business with people who already trust you, since the relationship is already established.

The big profits will always come from the current customer list, the repeat customers. They're the solid gold of your direct marketing business. Sure, you always have to have lead generation programs in place to bring new customers into the fold, but never, *never* forget your best customers. You have to treat them like kings and queens. Why? Because it costs so much money to get a new customer. Many years ago, for example, my colleague Russ von Hoelscher interviewed Howard Ruff, the newsletter publisher. Ruff was selling newsletter subscriptions to his *Rough Times* for about $99 each at that juncture. Russ asked Howard, "What does it generally cost you to get a new $99 subscription to your newsletter?" Ruff shot back immediately, "Almost $150 to get a $99 sale." Then he laughed and he said, "Yeah. It's a good way to lose money, isn't it, Russ?" Russ asked him, "So what's the secret, Howard?" Now, he had a pretty good idea what Mr. Ruff was going to say, but he explained it very well.

He said that although it cost about $50 of his own money to get a new subscriber, good customer service generally prompted them to buy additional books and services. He also had coins, gold, and other things he'd sell them. Plus, when they renewed their subscription for $99, it probably cost him less than $10-$12 to service that second-year subscription. He was willing to lose $50 in the beginning in order to get a new customer. That should open your eyes as to the value of a customer. Once you have a customer, you can continue to mail to them at a very low price.

People who've read a lot about direct response marketing, or who have been to a few seminars, know that one of the main success principles is to mail to your customers often -- but most people don't know what that really means. I think it's as simple as offering them special sales and new products that you develop especially for them. (Incidentally, that's **Secret Number Four**, the million-dollar formula that we're going to talk about in more detail later!)

You can find all kinds of things you can sell to your customers. That's what everybody wants to know: "What do I sell to my customers again and again?" The answer, simply enough, is to keep your eye out for related products

-- products like the ones you've sold them already. Develop new products in that vein. Go out to other entrepreneurs and ask them, "What do you have in this particular field and what kind of a good deal can you give me? I want to sell this to my customers." By doing this, you can get a constant flow of new products, services, books, or whatever the related product is because you want to continue to sell to a person who's likely to buy.

Whatever people buy habitually is the product you want to sell. That's a good, strong marketing concept. If somebody has a hobby or an interest, or they're buying some specific type of product, they're perfect candidates for buying more of that same kind of product. It's almost as if people have an insatiable need to continue to buy things. A gun collector won't be happy with just one gun; they have to have two, then four, and then eight. People who buy books on making money get into the habit of buying more. Like Eugene Swartz says, "If you're selling diet books, the mailing list you want is someone who's bought a diet book in the past 30 days." There are plenty of those kinds of lists out there and all kinds of media available for you to use to reach people.

Secret Number Four, which I alluded to a minute ago, is our million-dollar direct mail formula. It's the way we come up with winning products for the front end. Now, I don't know how we developed this; we may have read about it, or it may be a truly original idea. In any case, we use a simple four-step formula. One, we develop a product for our customers. Two, we write the sales letter or direct mail package. Three, we send it out to our best customers. Four, if our best customers go crazy over it (which means we make a lot of sales), we roll it out to the rest of our customers. Then we start testing to outside lists because we know that this is something our best customers were super-excited about -- which means that millions of other people will potentially be interested in it, too.

Once you get a customer and fulfill the order, put something extra in that order. A good catalog, brochure, or flyer will get you a lot of bounce-back orders. You're going to have a happy person if you're selling something good and inexpensive on the front end. So, the next thing to do, within two or three weeks (or less), is to send a solo mailing to that customer offering the related item. That customer has you fresh in their mind; hopefully they have warm and fuzzy thoughts about you because they like what you sent them in the first place. They're a great candidate to buy something else, if you mail to them quickly.

I don't want you to get the false idea about what I'm trying to say. A lot of the product ideas that we come up with just plain don't work. When we're just barely able to make a profit selling something to our best customers, we know that we have a dud on our hands. If the people who do the most business with us don't go absolutely crazy over it, nobody else will, either. But all we need is for about one out of every ten new ideas to work out really well. Then, by rolling it out to our customer base and doing what we call "fine tuning," you can roll out then to millions of other people and that's how to get rich. I'm going to talk a lot about the specific details of what "fine tuning" is in Part II of this publication.

The point is, if an idea won't work with your best customers, forget about trying to make it work with people who don't know you. One thing I need to add here is if it does work with your best customers, then you should test it again to the outside list before doing a full-fledged rollout. Sometimes things work well with your best customers, but not to the rest of the list -- and if you're foolish enough to do a full rollout, you can lose a lot of money. For some reason, those people who know you will buy from you and people who don't know you might scratch their heads and say, "I don't know." You never roll out with something until you've made it as good as you possibly can.

Secret Number Five is segmenting your customer list. One of the most important things that we ever did was to divide out our best customers from the rest of our customer base. Your best customers (the family jewels, as we call them) are the multiple buyers. They're the people who respond on a regular basis to your offers. They may not buy everything you send them or accept every offer that you make, but they buy consistently. They make three, four, five, or six purchases a year. They become your multiple buyers. They're the best of the best of the best. By putting them in a segment by themselves, they become your #1 source for testing new offers.

Then, behind them, but still very important, are the customers who make an occasional purchase from you. They're your customers on a somewhat irregular basis. Then, of course, you get down to the one-time customer who came in on a very low-priced offer. You might even have a few people who came in free. If you don't hear from such a customer after making repeat mailings to them, then they're really not your customer; they're just somebody who bit on a free offer. It quickly stops becoming profitable to mail to them.

Finally, you can also segment your list by different products that people buy and even by the amount of money they spend. At M.O.R.E. Inc. any customer who spends more than a certain dollar amount with us has proven that they're qualified to be in our group of "preferred customers." This also helps us get rid of the expensive people who don't buy anything. We decided, "Anybody who spends this much money with us has proven that they're qualified to be on our 'preferred customer' list. Anyone who spends less than this other amount we won't send any more mail to." Eventually, that last group has to be dropped from the list. That's the one technique that's meant more to us than anything. When we talk about making $400,000 in seven weeks, that's the group of customers that we made it from -- the frequent buyers.

It's all part of the 80-20 principle you hear so much about -- though I think it's more like 90-10. In any case, the idea is that a certain segment of your customers (it may be as few as 10%) become the multiple buyers, the people who buy 80%-90% of what you're selling. They're the customers who love you and your products and, of course, you should love them back. They're the ones who are the absolute core customers. They're your *best* customers. You've got to treat them like kings and queens. They're the ones who will tell you whether new offers are likely to work or not.

Secret Number Six is developing relationships with your customers. I know a lot of people are confused about that and want to know what it really means. Well, think of it this way: it means that the customer thinks about you as a real person, not as a faceless entity, and you think about them that way, too. You may not know each other personally, but still, you have a relationship. The way you develop that relationship is through your communications, whether it's by sales letters, postcards, brochures, or whatever you're using to reach that customer. You have a way to communicate with them that makes them realize you're a lot like them. My wife Eileen did that so well. People realize that *here* is a good woman in Kansas. Here's a woman who came from just a few steps above poverty and has climbed up to great success! She's a woman who wants to take thousands of people with her down the road of success. So, when Eileen communicates with people all over the country, they get the feeling that she's someone they can trust. Here's a real person to like.

I always try to do that myself. I try to be accessible by phone and email to let people know, "You're a real person and I'm a real person. I really care about you. I want to make money, but I also want to help you." Even when I'm not accessible, I have a whole staff of people who are. My staff will take the time to deal with anybody's problems. That's one thing that really helps out our customer base.

Think about most mail order companies, mail order dealers, and direct response marketers. I hate to say this, but I'm going to because it's true: they don't *want* to communicate with the customer. They won't take their phone calls or they don't have a staff dedicated to helping people. They want to keep everything at arm's length. Sometimes they don't even have a high regard for their customers. I know of several people who are selling garbage products and they're really scam artists. I've met them at various seminars or conventions. They have such a low opinion of their own products and such a low self-esteem. They also have a very low opinion of the people who buy from them -- and that's just a terrible way to do business.

You need to treat people right: give them good

products, give them good customer service, and be personable with them. Also, you need to develop a good offer that really applies to them. You can do it in a page or a postcard, or you may need a sixteen page sales letter that explains exactly what you're offering, what's really good about it, and how it can help the person who's reading it. Don't try to use all the hot buttons and tricks of a great ad writer. Just make a great offer in simple terms that a person can understand and respond to.

Always try to treat your customer as you want to be treated: that's one key to success. Another is staying in constant touch with customers so that they don't forget you. You should always be sending them something. A lot of people will hear this and say, "Well, my goodness, this is just simple common sense." Others will ask, "What does this have to do with direct mail?" You see, good customers are like money in the bank, but it's money that has to be mined. Everything you do to and for your customers helps build that relationship. You can't go see the customer like a salesperson would do and have that relationship built on a one-to-one basis; you use direct mail as a substitute for that.

Secret Number Seven is building or acquiring a good mailing list. Now, let's talk about what it actually takes to build a mailing list. This is something a lot of people are confused about. They hear that they should be mailing to their customers six or seven times a year and they hear that their customer mailing list is so vitally important that it's worth its weight in gold. But they don't know how to build it and it's crucial that they do so. The way to do it is to compile it from all the people who order from you or send inquiries to you. You build it from your ads in newspapers and magazines. You build it from postcard decks. You build it from anyone who gets in touch with you who wants information about your products or services. You build this mailing list, also, by doing direct mail to get other business. You use lists from other people. It's their list, but anyone who replies to you then can go on *your* list.

Now, I do want to offer a caveat here. When you use other people's mailing lists, make sure you're dealing with a good, reputable list broker. You should be getting names that are right for the offer you have. Stay away from cheap lists. Sometimes you'll open up an income or money-making opportunity magazine and find that people are offering very cheap lists. Well, years ago, I tested some of those lists. They didn't work well at all for me and they usually don't work well for anyone I talk to. Sure, they only cost $20-30 for a thousand addresses so people think, "What a bargain!" Well, when you throw in the cost of postage and printing, a cheap list that doesn't produce isn't a bargain. It ends up being very costly.

To find good mailing-list brokers with good lists, check with the SRDS: the Standard Rate and Data Service. They offer a manual that contains all the mailing lists in the country that are for rent -- or at least all the *reputable* lists. I'd say there are over 40,000 different lists in this huge directory, all broken down by market. You pick the market that you're most interested in (for us, it would be the opportunity seeker market) and check that section in the SRDS. You'll find a list of relevant lists, along with the names of the brokers or the list managers. You'll see the same names cropping up repeatedly in every market. There are several list management companies that are dominant in those markets.

That's the recommended way to find good lists. What's really exciting is that there are literally thousands of categories. You could be looking for health, diet, people who have bought books on losing weight, opportunity seekers, or whatever. Once you find names in those categories and find the list managers or brokers, you also get a pretty good idea as to how successful the promotion is. Somebody might say, "I have a list on 'How to Lose Fifty Pounds in Fifty Days.' Now, if you had a diet book and you find another list and find that in the last three months there are 25,000 names on that list, then you should also look into getting that diet book and seeing what's in it. See how you can modify your offer because the SRDS not only gives you all the lists that are available, but they also tell you something about how successful your competitors are. It's a great way to get inside information. Some of the brightest minds in direct response marketing go to the SRDS even before they start a new project to see, "How big is the universe? How many people have bought a product or service similar to what I want to sell?" That will tell you whether you want to go ahead with this project.

You'll find dominant list managers or brokers within every market. Those people possess inside information as to which lists are working for their clients. These people can make you a fortune because they know, out of all of the different opportunity lists, which ones are the most powerful, which ones work the best, and which ones make their clients the most money. They can steer you to those lists so that when you rent those lists and mail to them, you make a nice profit, too. If you're in the opportunity field, you have to know two names: Stuart Cogan in California with Mega-Media Associates (the group we use) and Howard Linzer of Macromark in New York City. These are two of the biggest players, the folks who can tell you which lists are working the best.

You'll also need to know the difference between a list manager and a list broker. A list manager is someone or some company that actually maintains your mailing list; a list broker is someone who works with the different list managers and brokers through these outside list managers. Some people are both; they go back and forth. You might have Stuart Cogan or Howard Linzer acting as managers of certain lists, but they can also act as brokers who can get you any list, even the ones they don't manage. Some companies are strictly list brokers; they can get any list on the market because they're part of a broker network. Others are list managers; they manage certain lists only.

Now, no matter where you get a list, you should test it to make sure it's going to work for your offer, especially if it's a new list. That brings me right into **Secret Number Eight**: the importance of testing. We do an amazing amount of testing at M.O.R.E., Inc. Sometimes people think that the direct response marketing business is like gambling and, yes, there's some truth in that. You can't know, from the beginning, which ads or sales letters are going to work the best. Some people look at this kind of marketing the same way they'd look at gambling with their money in Las Vegas. But that's *not* the way to look at it. If you test properly, you can spend very little money to find out whether your proposition is going to work or not. Testing is the key to getting rich. You find out what works and what doesn't.

Take, for example, a project we did a few years back. Since we were comfortable with the lists we used, we did a huge test -- 50,000 mailings. Now, I'd never recommend that to somebody new, but we've been doing direct mail in this particular market for a long time now so we know which lists are working. We tested ten different sales letters that all sold the same offer. It was a front-end offer that we were using to attract new customers. The only thing that was different about these letters was the front page. We tested new headlines, new front-page formats, and so forth, trying to find out which letter worked best. It was a first-class test, so the results came back very quickly -- in a matter of weeks. Just as we figured, one or two of those letters out-pulled the others by a five-to-one margin. Isn't that incredible? With that same offer, but with a different opening paragraph and a different headline, we created results which varied by 500%.

In that case, we also tested some different layout designs. Five of the letters had great big, bold headlines on them along with Eileen's picture; five of the letters had what's called a Johnson box, where there's no picture and no real headline to speak of. We found that the letters with Eileen's picture out-pulled the letters without it.

That brings me to another thing. You can test all kinds of things: not just headlines and copy, but also layout designs or the use of photographs versus no photographs. Any number of these things can significantly increase your response. Of course, I would have predicted that Eileen's photo would work because not only is she a good looking woman, but using a photo of the ad-writer personalizes things. Another thing you can test is letters with underline marks and colored text (especially red, green, or blue). We've done a lot of underlining. You can even test white paper against a colored stock; in fact the list of all the things you could test is endless.

The main thing to remember is that direct mail is a personal medium: it goes directly to people's homes. It's in their mailbox with the same good stuff that's coming from their friends and loved ones, the folks who send them letters, birthday cards, and so forth. Our mail goes right in that same mailbox where all that good stuff goes -- so the more you can make that direct mail look like personal mail, the better your chances are to get it opened. Among other things, you should always test a plain first-class mailing with nothing but the return address. Sometimes we use just the address and the state, not even the name.

One more thing I'd like to point out before we go on to the next secret is this: many of the best list brokers and managers make you take at least 5,000 names from any category on any list that you're renting. That's okay; you don't have to mail to all of them, especially if you're starting on a limited budget. In fact, it's a bad idea if you have no idea as to the actually quality of the names. The broker might have told you that these names are great and he might really believe that. If you take those 5,000 names and mail to 2,000 of them and get a good response, you can mail to the other 3,000. If you don't get a good response mailing to 2,000 (or even as few as 1,500), you can throw the rest of them out. This has saved many of our clients money when they were in the start-up mode. Remember: if you have a product to sell, don't assume you're going to do great with a list just because someone else did. Try mailing to one-third of those names and, based on that, decide whether to mail the rest of them.

Let's say you do that, and your promotion really

works. Well, **Secret Number Nine** is rolling out the product. Rolling out is the thing that can really make you rich. Here's how it works. Let's say we test a few thousand names each from ten different lists. Let's say, as often happens, that three of them work really well, two of them so-so, and five of them, frankly, just don't work very well at all. Now, what we want to do is consider a roll out with the three that work. That doesn't mean that if the lists are big (thirty, forty, or fifty thousand), we're going to take all the names. Some people get a good test and when they go back for more names, they get bombed. So, let's say we mailed a few thousand and it worked well. We'd go back then with 5,000 or 10,000 of the 30,000 names that (in this particular example) are available. If that worked, we'd go get the rest of the names and do the complete roll out. With the marginal lists, we'd probably try to get a couple thousand more mailed just to retest it. If it seemed to work a little better, we'd start to take more from those lists. Of course, if the lists don't work well in our test, just forget about them.

This is one of the reasons I happen to think that this is the world's perfect business. It's the only business I know of that you can actually lose money on nine different things and still make a fortune on that one thing that works, the one thing that you can roll out with. Think back to the example I provided earlier, where we were testing ten different front pages. When you do a test like that, you're hoping to find one superstar, the best of the best. When you do, the other nine can be discarded and you can proceed with the one that does five times better than the others. That's a lot better than just taking the best idea we have and running with it because it looks good. We might end up missing out on five times the money we could actually make.

The key to making millions of dollars is as simple as making hundreds of dollars. If you can make $100 net profit from mailing 1,000 pieces of mail, then you know that you've got something very powerful. That same $100 grows to $10,000 when you mail 100,000 pieces, and $100,000 for every million pieces that you put in the mail. For example: I worked with a guy in Seattle many years ago who was making an offer to show people who'd just gotten their real estate licenses how to be better real estate salesmen. He did a small sample mailing to about 200 of those new licensees, all on his own. It wasn't a very good sales letter and it was a very small sample.

He called me up later and said, "You know, we made about $125 and, of course, that's not very good. But I guess there's some interest in this." I asked him, "How many people get their licenses in real estate?" This was back in the late 1970s or early 1980s. He told me, "Well, nationwide, I think in any given year there might be 300,000 or 350,000." I told him, "You're going to make a lot of money. If you mailed to 200 people and made $125, Katie-bar-the-door! Use a better sales letter and with mass mailings done by a mailing house, there's going to be no limit on the profits." He went on to make hundreds of thousands of dollars. So like I said, the key is to find out how to make a hundred dollars. You can easily then make $100,000, $200,000, $300,000 and more. It's the exact opposite of gambling. Find out how to make a little profit and then just multiply yourself.

Secret Number Ten is to use inexpensive direct mail. At the beginning of this publication I discussed how direct mail can encompass all kinds of things. Some of the more inexpensive types of direct mail include postcards, inquiry-generated letters, and similar products.

The postcard is one of the best vehicles to use for lead generation. You have to make a very inexpensive or free offer. You tell them just to return the card to you, with their name and address, or to call a phone number and give their name and address. A lot of people use the double postcard (which is twice as big) to sell front-end projects in the $15-25 range, but I still think the postcard should be used for inexpensive or free offers. My own experience tells me that that is better. Also, there are card packs offered by companies like Advo, Venture Communication, and Doyle Publishing that go to hundreds of thousands of people. You're not really doing the direct mail, then; you're just supplying an ad they can mail out.

An inquiry-generating letter is very simple: it's a small sales letter that's usually just two to four pages and includes some type of an ordering device. It could be an order form or just a response card where the customer fills their name out and sends it back. We use a lot of inquiry-generating type of letters to go out to people we've never done any business with. We make it very easy for those people to send us a small amount of money or to show us in some other way that they're interested in our offer. This is another inexpensive way to mail because you don't have all the long sales letters, the list pieces, and all the circulars and brochures and that type of thing to deal with.

Postcards or inquiry-generating letters are the best ways to generate leads. The power of it is that you're mailing to people who don't know you. When you make them a great offer for just a few bucks or you offer them a report absolutely free, they're not afraid to invest in getting to know you. It's only going to cost a couple bucks or it's going to be FREE. That is how you can build confidence. Of course, then, the key to success is to send them a very compelling sales message or sales letter immediately once you receive their inquiry.

One of the things that we do to make sure that we convert them is to offer something we call a "marriage offer." This is to make sure we're getting inquiries that we can turn a nice profit on when we sell whatever we have on the back-end. A "marriage offer" is very similar to the sales piece that we send people when they respond. It's like that front-end lead generation message that we're sending out to attract those new customers. What happens is that the customer is already half-sold when they send us that initial $5, $10, or $20 or even when the customer just sends back the card saying, "Yes, I'm interested." We've qualified those customers because the package that we send out is very similar to the one they responded to in the first place. The key is to send it quickly. I'm amazed, when working with some direct mail clients, to learn that they only mail out their follow-ups once a week -- or every couple weeks. This is nonsense. If you get an inquiry on Monday, the response should be in the mail no later than Tuesday morning. That's something that we've done from Day One. That's the one thing we refuse to test. We refuse to hold onto an order for a couple of weeks and see how much less response we get. I know that that's partially responsible for our success. You don't have to test that one; that's written in gold. The faster you respond, the more confidence you build in your potential customer.

Secret Number Eleven we learned from a book called *Secrets of Direct Mail* by Dick Benson. In that book, Dick talks a lot about costs of mailing versus how much money you can make. One of the things he says is that it doesn't matter how much a mailing costs. Many times you can spend more money on a mailing and generate a lot more than you could by trying to cheapen it up or by trying to cut corners, like so many people new to this business try to do. It's too common in this business for people do everything on the CHEAP. They get the cheapest names, they get the cheapest printer, they use the cheapest envelopes, or they buy plain envelopes and stamp them with a rubber stamp. They do things that just shout out to the potential buyer, "Small time," "Ma and Pa," "Watch out! This is a very rinky-dink dealer." It's such a crying shame because that's going to prevent them from getting orders.

This is one of the world's perfect businesses because you *can* just be a small one-person company working from your kitchen table. But you can present the image of being a huge company just by doing a few simple things like using high-quality paper and working with a good graphic artist. There are very simple things that can be done that can give people the impression that you're much bigger than you actually are. It pays rich dividends. Nobody wants to deal with someone who looks like they're just a little part-timer. Even though there's nothing wrong with that, especially in the beginning, you don't want to shout that from the rooftop to all your potential buyers. You want to look like a big, well-established company.

Here's another helpful factor: give your business and individual products good names. Here's an example of something a fellow named Ben Swarn did. Many years ago, he started an astrological association called the American Association of Astrologers -- and at the beginning he was just working in his basement in Canton, Ohio. What happened is it became a huge organization, but it started with those humble beginnings and he gave it a good name. So, giving your company or your products great names is important. Using good letterheads and good printing to put forth a good image is also crucial. If you're selling a high-priced item, you want that initial sales package that goes out to your customers to have really nice stuff, a nice cover letter or a nice brochure. This is to make yourself look like you're worth sending that money to.

One of the ways we've done that at M.O.R.E., Inc. is by means of **Secret Number Twelve**: working with a good mailing house. A lot of people don't even know what a mailing house is. First of all, there are mailing houses in almost every city in the country. We're here in the middle of nowhere, Goessel, Kansas, and within an hour's drive of here, we have huge mail houses. All you have to do is look in the phonebook under "Advertising Direct Mail." These companies can do all kinds of things to help give your direct mail a good, solid look. They'll stuff envelopes for you mechanically and put them straight into the mail. A lot of people think, "Well, that must be expensive." I recently talked to a client who just did a 10,000-piece mailing -- just himself, his wife, and his sister-in-law stuffing envelopes and mailing them out. He was telling me that he was bone-tired and was so upset because it was just a mountain of work. I told him about a letter shop, a mailing house, that could do the work for him. He went and saw them. He found out that he could have gotten the job done for the same price, or less, and it could have been done in one day -- instead of the week he, his wife, and his sister-in-law spent at it, working their fingers to the bone.

Now, you do need to watch everything closely. You can't turn over your pieces to a mail house without keeping an eye on them. There seem to be some black holes in the United States Postal Service system and, of course, you need to keep an eye on your mailing house and how they handle things. Until you really know your mailing house, you have to keep checks and balances with them -- and even once you do get to know them, it doesn't hurt to check things occasionally to make sure everything's still working smoothly.

Part II: How to Do It

In the last section, I covered twelve principles of direct mail marketing and now I'm going to cover the other thirteen. The real difference is this section is that I'm going to show you exactly what you have to do to put together all you learned in Part I. Remember, these are the same ideas that have made us and thousands of other people around the country millions of dollars. So let's get right to it, shall we?

Secret Number 13 is simply this: become familiar with direct mail math. Direct mail math is very simple: all it involves is adding up the cost to get out a mailing. The two chief components of that cost are usually postage and printing. Now, if you run an office with employees like I do, then you do get into overhead and a few other expenses. But basically it all comes down to postage, printing, and perhaps the rental of mailing lists. When you add up the cost, usually, you do it per thousand. How much does it cost you to mail a thousand pieces of direct mail? That amount could be $400 or $500; it could be more determined, in part, by whether you're mailing first-class mail or by bulk-rate mail. You just multiply up the numbers; you know exactly what it costs to put a thousand pieces in the mail even if you're mailing five, ten, or twenty thousand pieces.

The other side of the direct mail equation is: How many orders do you get per thousand and how much gross income do they bring in? Then you go a little bit farther and look at how much it costs to fulfill every order. How much does it cost to ship the book, the product; how much is postage, and what's the cost of the envelope? What does it cost to get that order to the customer? So you add up how much it costs to mail, add up the results, and then add up how much it costs to fulfill. Of course, if you don't know the results at first, you still can do direct mail math, just by determining how many orders you'll need to cover your expenses. This way you always know exactly what you have to do to generate a profit; you always know where you're at. You can look at the numbers every single day. Around our shop, we sometimes watch the numbers every hour or two when we're doing a big promotion. We take a lot of phone orders so we always know exactly where we're at all times. That's crucial.

If you have a lead generation program where you're giving a free report away, or charging a very nominal fee for a report, tape, or whatever, then of course the direct mail math switches into a different mode, one where your profits have to come out of the back-end. But again, it's just a matter of doing the math; it's just simple addition, subtraction, and multiplication. You know exactly where you are at all times. That's exciting because it allows you to make decisions on whether to roll out or pull back and rework the package. And then, usually, after you get the whole thing put together, you have a formula where you know that a return envelope cost you this much money and the sale flyer costs you *this* much money. Then you just keep that formula in all your future direct mail packages, as long as costs remain steady. It becomes very easy, after you do this for a while, to know exactly what your costs are.

Because direct mail math is all simple, basic math, it also helps remind you of how crucial it is that you buy your envelopes and your printing at the lowest possible price, while maintaining good quality. That's crucial: you *must* maintain good quality. Avoid false economy, but don't be afraid to shop around -- because if you can save $50 on printing per thousand and you eventually roll out with 100,000 pieces, that's $5,000 saved. Money saved can be money earned. Even if you only save a penny on each piece, you're talking about some serious money if you're sending out 100,000 pieces in a mailing.

One more thing about direct mail math: when you decide to price your product and services, you should test the market by using different prices. Several years ago, our friend Russ von Hoelscher put out a real estate offer (a manual and some tapes) and tested them at $49.95, $59.95, $69.95, and $79.95. He was amazed to learn that $69.95 was by far the most profitable offer. He did get more orders at $49.95, but not enough to compensate for that extra $20. The surprising thing was $69.95 did much better than $59.95; not just with profit, but with many more orders. So always test, test, test -- and price testing is one of the most important things to test. You'll be amazed, sometimes, how you might have to lower your price to get the most orders and to get the overall best return. Many other times, you'll be amazed to find that you can charge much more than you thought you could!

The key is to get something going very small. Again, test it slowly so you're not investing a whole lot of money in your direct mail campaigns. You're just spending a little at a time and finding what works. Then, know that when you roll out, part of direct mail math is figuring out how many millions of dollars you can make. That's what's *really* exciting. If you have an offer that works to 5,000 people and makes you even $500, that's exciting because if there's a potential universe out there for your products -- and by universe we simply mean if there's potentially, let's say, a million people out there that you can mail it to -- then you just can start multiplying that $500 per 5,000 all the way up to a million. Of course, there are variances. Some lists work better than others.

There's just no end in sight of what you can do once you find something that's profitable. Basically, what I'm saying is that you need to get your fulfillment costs down. You need to get your mailing costs down and keep track of those so you can find your break-even point. With us, sometimes it's 100 or 200 orders before we finally break even. Once we pass that mark, then it's all profits -- except for fulfillment. It all gets back to something I talked about in Part I. Figure out a way to make $50 or $100. With direct mail, you could actually take that to

$100,000. You could take it to $1,000,000, as long as the mailing list universe is big enough to handle extensive mailing.

Secret Number Fourteen is creating powerful offers. This has a great deal to do with the success of any direct mail campaign. In direct mail, the mailing list you use (whether it's yours or an outside list that you rent) is your single most important component; but next to it, there's nothing more powerful than making a good offer. A good offer has something to do with a good product and service, but it goes beyond that. It means that you actually format an offer that's easy to understand, that's exciting, that's motivating, that gives all kinds of benefits to the reader, and excites and motivates them to head for their checkbook or to grab their Visa or MasterCard.

If you learn to make powerful offers, there's no limit on how much money you can make. The secret is to study the good mailing pieces of others in the field. Get as many books as you can on the subject of direct mail. Read some of my other publications. Also, subscribe to certain newsletters on direct marketing. Learn how to craft an offer because there's nothing more important. Think of the customer. Think of what his wants and desires are. Think about how to make a proposition that's irresistible. Make it so you feel that the person just can't turn this down if they're interested in the subject matter at all. And of course, your mailing list should be targeted only to people who are likely to be interested.

Here are a few important points about crafting an offer. First of all, you need to make your offer very reader-friendly. Have an envelope enclosed with the offer. Have an 800-number where they can call and place an order. Make it really easy for them to order. I believe the order form should always be separate from the sales letter or the brochure. Make it easy for them so they don't have to cut it with a scissors or anything; they can just take it and mail it.

Next, you need a powerful headline or lead statement. Now, when we talk headlines, we're usually talking about ads, but I've found (and many others have, too) that you can use a headline in a sales letter. You put a big, powerful headline up there, then drop down and start with the regular letter. It works like a Rolex. What should your headline be? Oftentimes, it should be something to do with "How-to" -- that's a proven formula for making money using ads or sales letters. For example: "How to Make $5,000 a Week" or "How to Look Ten Years Younger in Thirty Days."

You can also use a news headline and you can keep in mind who, what, when, where, why and how, the classic newspaper approach. You can also tell a story. This is something that you may not want to do at first, but if you study how other people have done it, you can learn to tell a story. By telling a story, I mean a personal, *truthful* story about how you came to make this offer to your customer. Tell something of your past, keeping it interesting: what you've learned, what you've discovered, what came to motivate you to write this person today. Telling a story can be very powerful and it can really make the offer personal. Then, make a bold statement: "Pay Zero Taxes," for example, is a bold statement if you can back it up with your copy. Anything that hits the person over the head and captures their attention makes a good headline.

This brings us to **Secret Number Fifteen**: writing dynamite ad copy. I've already mentioned the importance of a headline and how it can even be used in the sales letter. Now, if you don't use a headline in the sales letter but you want to keep it completely personalized, then you need a very powerful, compelling copy in the opening statement which becomes something like a headline. The key to writing good copy is to stress benefits. Have a lot more "you's" than "I's." Really put yourself in the mindset of the reader, try to push their buttons, and get them motivated by what you're saying. You do that by stressing the benefits completely. Just lay out as many benefits as you can.

Try to keep it personalized. Talk to that person. You might be sending out 100,000 direct mail pieces, but you should be dealing with each person who's reading your letter with a one-to-one approach. A sales letter *always* goes into a direct mail package, even if you have flyers and other brochures in that package. The letter is still the most important. Don't split your message. If you have flyers in there, as well as the sales letter, make your top benefits and your top pitch be in both the sales letter and the flyer. You want to keep things consistent; people don't like big paragraphs and they don't like long sentences. Keep it short!

Whenever possible, offer some freebies. People love to get something for free. If you're selling something for $100, $500, or $50, whatever the price is, you can offer some paper-and-ink freebies, at least a couple of them, and they'll cost you maybe twenty-five cents each. This will always enhance the return because people like to get those bonuses. All the bonuses have to be in some short report format, as long as they have good information in them. Another important thing is to use testimonials whenever possible because people like to know what other people say about your product or service. Another key element with a sales letter is a postscript -- a P.S. With the exception of the introduction or headline to the sales letter, nothing gets read more than the P.S. *Always* add a postscript to every sales letter.

Remember that good sales letter writing is just salesmanship in print. You're telling the prospect (or the customer, because a lot of our mailings are to existing customers) about all of the things that are in it for them, communicating that to them in the best possible way. I realize a lot of people are afraid of writing. I was; I used to be extremely scared of it. But a lot of people go about it the wrong way in the beginning. I think that when most people think about writing ads or sales letters, they think about the vehicle too much. They think, perhaps, about how they have to be clever. They have to be smart. They have to be shrewd. They have to somehow *trick* somebody into buying their product or service. Well, this is absolutely balderdash. Nothing can be further from the truth! The secret to writing a dynamite sales letter is simply to be honest and friendly, but nevertheless, to stress all the big benefits. Anyone can learn to write good sales copy, if they just remember this: you just want to communicate with people pretty much the way you would across the back fence or how you would if you were sitting down talking to somebody over a cup of coffee.

Forget about being cute. Forget about being shrewd. Forget about trying to trick somebody into ordering, or using all the hype and all the magical words like "amazing" and "tremendous." Sure, sometimes we use these words, but only in their proper contexts. The main thing is to communicate very honestly. Stress the benefits. Come across very sincerely, yet be enthusiastic. You can write a great sales letter without considering yourself to be a great copywriter. Some copywriters make the mistake of trying to be brilliant when they write when, actually, the key to success is to be down-to-earth and honest. Too many times I've seen sales letters that are too crowded; there's no white space on them. Well, sales letters need to be "reader-friendly."

Secret Number Sixteen involves the outer envelopes. For years and years, I've believed and I've preached a plain-Jane simple white #10 envelope. That's the standard business envelope. It's the best. Don't use teaser copy on it. Many great copywriters believe that way, though others believe that teaser copy can work. I've come to realize that in many cases, I'm right -- that plain-Jane envelope was best. For other offers, some great copywriters have done a great job by smearing the whole front of a 6 x 9 or a 9 x 12 large envelope with about fifty benefits. Sometimes that's worked. Rodale Press, which publishes *Prevention* magazine and a lot of health books, is fantastically successful with this approach. Some of the Stock and Gold newsletter financial publishers also use a lot of teaser copy -- so you really have to test both approaches. I think if you're mailing first-class, and you're mailing with a live 42-cent stamp or the imprint (that is, you're going through the meter), I think it's still best to use the regular, white envelope and just have an address as a return. Don't even include a name. Then, put the customer's name, address, city, state, and zip on the envelope. You should definitely test both plain and teaser copy envelopes when sending bulk mail.

We've found that with our front-end direct mail packages, it's better to use no teaser copy, just a plain envelope. With our customer base, we always have my photograph, sometimes we'll put teaser copy on it, and it works pretty well. That's because when you're mailing to your customers and have a good relationship with them, you want them to know this mailing is coming from you.

Plus, we spend more money on envelopes for our existing customers. In fact, with our best customers, we'll spend tremendous amounts of money per thousand because it's an investment for us. These are people we've established a relationship with so we can spend a more money to reach them with a first-class offer. I'm talking about a *huge* sales letter. A lot of the envelopes we use for our customers are the hard envelopes, the expensive kind that look just like Federal Express envelopes. These are called "Direct Mail Express" or "Urgent Response" envelopes and they're very colorful; sometimes they'll even have eagles on them. They look like UPS or Federal Express envelopes and are coming on the scene more and more. They pull very well because they capture people's attention. Although you may be just mailing first-class or bulk rate, many of the people getting these envelopes think they're receiving an overnight communication.

Secret Number Seventeen is lay-out. It's important, as I've already mentioned, to have a congruent letter that seems to flow. That is, it needs to have short paragraphs, short sentences, and a lot of white space to make it "reader-friendly." I think that's the key to success with a sales letter, especially a long one. People ask us, "Will people read a 12- or 16-page letter?" The answer is "Yes," as long as that letter is reader-friendly. If a customer looks at it and sees a whole mess of type with hardly any breaks, most will say, "I'm not buying into this." If it looks easy to read, people *are* going to read it - - especially if the opening sentence and the headline capture their attention.

We like to circle certain ideas in our letters with a color that's different from the text color. We underline things to make them stand out. We do things to make our letters look personable. Now, the customer's not ignorant; they know these letters were printed out by the thousands by huge printing presses. Still, we try to do things to make our letters look friendly by using handwritten notes in the margins and similar methods that give it a personal feel. Also, we work with a good graphic artist. This has been one of the things that has helped us more than anything - - working with somebody who understands the importance of how to lay things out to make them look the best.

Plus, we get lots of ideas by looking at other people's mailings. It's common for people to throw away direct mail; they call it junk mail. When you're in the business, though, you should *never* throw your direct mail away. This is how we get some of our best ideas -- by studying other people's mail. That's the concept of the swipe file, which is something you should institute immediately when you start in this business. You should especially take a close look at mail you get over and over again because that's how you know they're successful. Whatever they're doing is working, so you want to look at how they craft the offer. You want to know what type font they're using, along with the range of variances. How does their entire direct mail piece look to you? You can learn a lot from that because you don't study failure. You want to study *success*.

A lot of companies that do direct mailings -- especially the ones that send out letters about subscribing to financial newsletters, newsletters on gold and silver, or newsletters on stock market and mutual funds -- spend huge amounts of money on the very best freelance graphic artists. They test dozens of different approaches, trying to find the one that works the best. Even though I've been doing this myself for so many years, I continue to learn from the approaches of these newsletter publishers. They're using very sharp copywriters and they're using a very strong, hard sale. It takes a very strong sale for a newsletter. Whenever you can get any information on newsletter offers, save them because they're among the best.

Russ von Hoelscher is a member of the NRC, the National Republican Committee, and he tells me he gets letters from them at least three times a week. Every one of their letters is made out the same way. It's very clear and precise. You can get it, see exactly what they want, and what the money is going for. You know they're spending gobs and gobs of money to have those letters written. It's amazing, really, how the Republican Party is really up on direct mail. I believe they've hired some of the best talent available because I, too, am getting three and four approaches a week. They're sending me the Dollar Bill Letter, which is an eye-grabber. Here's how that works: you staple a dollar bill to the sales letter. This, incidentally, is something that, on short mailings or small mailings, you can do, too. It's costly, but if the offer is high-priced enough, the results are just amazing. Some of the best direct mail I'm receiving is coming from Conservatives and the Republican Party. They've apparently learned a lot.

Now, on to **Secret Number Eighteen** which is working with printers. This involves finding a good, competent printer who does what he says he'll do at a good price. You should constantly be checking with different printers because you want quality; but in direct marketing, you also have to have good price. The difference between printers can be the difference between twelve noon and midnight. Some are, quite literally, charging two and three times as much as others. You really need to shop, shop, shop, and find those printers with the different capabilities. They don't all do the same things. Sales letters are one thing, brochures another, books yet another -- so find the right printer for the job that needs done. There are some printers who can give us the best price for short runs, which is great, since we do lots of small tests. Then, on roll outs, where we're mailing 50,000-100,000 pieces at a time, there are printers that can give us better prices for *those* jobs. So you need to have a wide variety of printers to work with -- and always go for the ones that can give you the best service, reasonably good quality, and, of course, low price.

One more thing before we move on. When Eileen and I first started, we knew nothing about working with printers at all. The first printers we worked with were quick printers. First of all, we had a cash flow problem; we didn't have very much money. What we would do is this: every day we would get orders, and when we needed some more sales letters or whatever, we took all the money we had to spend that day, went up to the quick printer, and they turned these jobs around for us super fast. This is a great tip for small jobs: there are printers out there that can do very fast work for you and turn it around in a matter of hours. Sometimes they'd print our sales letters while we waited. As you grow, you'll need other printers that can do other jobs. For instance, we have book printers whose specialty is printing 500 to 1,000 books. We have *other* book printers whose specialty is printing 5,000 to 10,000. That's the key: to find the printer that can do the job. The instant printer is for something you need quickly. The printer who can do a brochure for you may take a little longer, but they do a good job at a reasonable price. Then, you may need different printers for booklets, manuals, or perfect-bound books.

Secret Number Nineteen is to use guaranteed space ads that you know will pull. Whenever you run an ad, you have to tie up your money six to eight weeks in advance unless you can get credit. All that time, you never really know if the ad is going to perform or not. One of the things that we've done is test all kinds of headline ideas through direct mail. We can test different offers and different story formats. Through testing these things, we find out what works best and then we develop our space ads around those ideas so that we already know exactly what's already proven to make us the most money. We utilize those ideas in our space ads.

If you have a good sales package that's working in direct mail, it's always a good idea to take its best points and then add a very good headline to them when you start crafting a space or display ad. If it's working well in direct mail, there's a good chance that you can make it work in space. This takes some of the risk away because space ads can be very risky. You put up a lot of money and then wait for weeks or months for it to appear. You're rolling the dice, in a sense. But once you know something's working in direct mail, you can condense that copy and there's a very good opportunity, if you pick the right publications, that you'll have a good space ad. Now, I want to say that with a space ad (you've heard this before, but I want to hammer it into your mindset), the headline is crucial. It's at least 50% or 60% of the value of the entire potential pulling power of the ad; some display ad experts even say 70% or 80. So, experiment with headlines in your direct mail. When you find the best one, try it in the space ad.

I want to tell a little story here. When we first started out in this business, somebody came up to me and said, "I saw your full page ad. That ad must have pulled in millions of dollars." One thing you need to understand is that one ad *cannot* pull in millions of dollars. You're lucky to get ten or twenty times the ad cost and even that's very unusual. Often if you get double your ad cost, it's successful. So, you need to place more than one ad in different magazines. You have to realize that it's a process and this idea of getting rich on one ad -- or on one direct mail campaign -- isn't realistic.

Secret Number Twenty is this: good copywriters can make you rich. Now, there are a lot of copywriters out there that specialize in mail order and direct mail. Some of these copywriters, like Russ von Hoelscher, don't come cheap, so if you're starting on a shoestring budget, you can't really hire a copywriter. But once your business has progressed to the point where you're making some money, or if you're starting a business with some capital, it's smart to get a good copywriter if you feel you don't know enough to do it yourself. *Don't* go to a local ad agency. You're likely to get a direct mail package or space ad that will absolutely bomb, mostly because it's not set up to appeal to a nationwide market. You have to find a good direct response copywriter. You can check in various publications like *DM News* to query two, three, or four of them. Pick the one whose budget you can handle and whom you're compatible with. A good copywriter won't cost you money; they'll make you money.

Also, they'll add leverage to your business. When you're doing everything, you don't have time to really sit down, study, and learn how to write all the ads yourself. If you hire an outside copywriter to help you on certain advertisements or sales pieces, that adds a lot of leverage to your business. Keep this in mind, too. A good copywriter should use his talents and make money for himself, but also, in many cases, he can do just as good or an even better job for you because he looks at things from afar -- he's not too close to the trees to realize that he's in a forest. A good copywriter will pay for himself.

Some copywriters offer a service called critiquing and this can be something that can make you a lot of money. Most do this fairly inexpensively because the same level of work and effort isn't required for them to sit down and critique a piece of copy, whether it's a sales letter, a space ad, or card deck. This is where we've saved a lot of money at M.O.R.E., Inc. Many times, one of the best copywriters will charge $400 or $500 to look the piece over and make a couple of recommendations. Those two or three recommendations can make you many thousands of dollars, *even* tens of thousands of dollars, over a period of time.

For example, if you want to get Russ von Hoelscher on the cheap, the best way to do it is to send him ads or direct mail packages that are already out there where he can critique them and tell you how to make them better. You can get small ads critiqued by him for less than $200, full page ads for less than $300, and direct mail packages for $400. It's a good way to get expert advice at ten cents on the dollar. It definitely worked wonders for us. When we starting working with Russ, we wrote our own full page ad. We spent many sleepless nights putting that thing together, then we sent it to him to critique and he made some fantastic adjustments to it.

While we've always liked to have as much control over everything as possible here at M.O.R.E. Inc., I don't recommend that for everyone. For some people that would be a terrible thing, though Eileen and I have strived since day one to learn how to write copy ourselves and to learn these skills that are necessary in direct mail communication. One of the problems that we've had since the beginning, though, is being able to go to people that we haven't done business with and to be able to bring in sales. We've been somewhat ineffective at that, to tell you the truth, and have been forced many times to use outside copywriters because we haven't been able to write to those prospects. I don't know exactly why that is, but once we have a customer we've done business with, I suppose it just feels easier for us to write copy to those people. Quite possibly, it stems from the very personal way we write copy. Our method clearly works best when we're writing to people who have done business with us, that have a relationship with us. When we go out to outside markets, we have to take a different approach. Then, once we bring them in as customers, we can go back to them in this more personal way.

Maybe it's the fact, too, that the new customers that we're trying to bring over into our customer base think our letters are hokey because we're too down-home. But whatever the reason, the fact is that we use a lot of different copywriters to do our front-end pieces. Some of these copywriters do a better job than we could ever do ourselves. They make us money, paying for themselves many, many times over. We're constantly running new promotions that bring new customers in, but once that's accomplished, we take it from there. On the back end, we handle all of our promotions. But have no doubt about it: Copywriting is hard work. If you can afford it, pay someone to critique your work, or even write those promotions you have trouble with.

Secret Number Twenty-One is the power of pyramiding your direct mail profits. This is where people get rich. It's simple, really: you just find something that works and then you take those profits and use them to make *more* profits. You get your cash flow flowing right through your business. Now, the key to that is to not spend the money as it comes in. Some people immediately want to spend the money that comes in and buy things that they've been looking forward to getting their hands on. Instead, at least in the beginning, pyramid the profits. If you can roll over every dollar of profit and hopefully double it in a set period of time, it's easy to see how you can go from a small investment to a small profit to a larger profit to, eventually, a gigantic profit. The way to do that is to pyramid the money. That's why you shouldn't quit your job and jump into this business. Start spare time, on a small basis, while you still have another job -- so you don't have to take the money out of your direct marketing business in the first several months.

We've always taken 30% out of every dollar that came in and set it aside for advertising so we can just keep that river flowing. We've run two checkbooks where one is just for our advertising budget. I don't even know how we got the idea for doing that; it's something that's always helped us more than anything else because we make sure, on a daily basis, that there's always plenty of money to put back into the advertising, which is going to make us even more money. It's exactly the opposite of gambling. Gambling is where you take something, cross your fingers, throw it out there, and hope it works. All those people who wish they could run an ad in the *National Enquirer*, with its six million readers, and think that a million people are just going to send them a buck -- well, that's gambling. They never know if their product will even sell in the *National Enquirer*. Their ideas aren't based on these good, solid principles I'm trying to teach here. People think, "Gee, the *National Enquirer* has six million readers. Now, if I can just get one out of a hundred of them to send me $20..." Of course, it never works out that way for a tiny ad. You go by bottom line profits. Don't get this pie-in-the-sky idea that if ten million people each would send you $2 you'll have twenty million dollars because that's not realistic.

Speaking of bottom line profits, **Secret Number Twenty-Two** is something that's made us huge amounts of profits. The secret is renting out our mailing list. When we first got started, we established a contact with a mailing list manager. In six years we generated over $500,000 in cash and it's only grown since then. The nice part about this is almost all that money has been pure profit for us because we've *already* made a profit on the mailing list. Anything over and above that just goes straight to our pockets.

Anybody can do this. Once you have at least 3,000-5,000 names, you can make some serious money on the side -- just by making your names available to a list broker who will rent them out to other companies. When you get a check from them, almost all of it is pure profit. No matter what market you're in, there are specific list managers who you should be working with. If you get your list up with the right manager, they'll do a very good job working around the clock. Our list manager is on the West Coast. Sometimes I've called him late at night and he'll still be there working. Because there's an hour difference, I'll call him at six o'clock in the morning and he'll be there working. (I'll forget that he's two hours behind us.) The point is that he works around the clock renting our mailing list out for us, doing all kinds of work, and we don't have to do anything but make sure that the names we send him are the very best names. Of course he keeps a percentage, but it doesn't cost you anything -- he takes it out of your profit.

In our experience, the key to a good mailing list is this: first of all, put together the very best names possible.

In other words, only put up your buyers' names on the lists you rent out. We don't put up any inquiry names, only the names of people who spent a certain dollar amount with us. Second, when we do take new customers, we do such a good job at trying to satisfy those new customers that I feel like they're more open and receptive when other companies rent our mailing list. That's why these companies keep coming back again and again to rent our list, because the people on that list are happy, satisfied, and willing to buy from other people.

It's also important to maintain a list of names that you won't rent to anyone, no matter what. As I mentioned in Part I, it's vital to segment your mailing list. You take your very best customers and you keep them separate from your other customers. *You don't want to give your best customers away to any other company.* You can make so much more money by doing individual marketing campaigns to those people.

Secret Number Twenty-Three is keeping a swipe file, something I've mentioned already. There are so many good ideas out there. Sometimes people say, "How do you guys come up with all your ideas?" Well, the truth is that we're not geniuses. Every time we see anything that's of any value that *somebody else* has put together, we save it in what we call a swipe file and we use as many of those ideas as we can in our own stuff. The swipe file is one of the keys to direct mail success because you want to know what other people in your particular industry are doing. It's exciting to get the mail, but you have to organize and categorize it, otherwise you go crazy. I used to throw it in boxes and then eventually I'd go crazy trying to look for a certain piece because it was buried with 300 other pieces. Try to keep things in order, but absolutely save the mail and look over what all these other offers are so that you can structure your own offer better. Don't copy them word for word; heavens, no. Just try to glean a few good points and ideas from some of the best letters. There are so many out there that you can adapt to your own use.

Here's what I mean. Some copywriters have charged companies $10,000, $15,000, and more to write their material -- and some have earned even more for their work. A lot of those full page ads you'll see rerunning over and again in the major tabloids, like the *Enquirer*, the *Globe*, and the *Examiner*, are written by copywriters who are paid not only their base pay but also residual income they get off any profits. Sometimes these writers are paid well over $100,000 for writing a full page ad! So these are the very best of the best ads that are out there. From the headline ideas and the layout ideas, there's just so much good material that can be learned. With a swipe file, you'll have the benefit of looking at their copy, studying it, and, perhaps, picking out a key point here or there to use in your own offers -- and you don't pay them a cent. So it's a very, very smart idea to have a swipe file of other people's ideas around.

Secret Number Twenty-Four is to make effective use of the USPS, the United States Postal Service. I know a lot of people say bad things about the Post Office, but we love them -- mostly -- because we've made so much money by using their service. There are some problems, though, so in a way you could say it's something of a love-hate relationship. The people that work for them are basically good people; however, the system is flawed, I think, simply because they're often not in touch as much as they should be with their customers on a national basis. Yet, with all their problems, they do a better job than just about any other postal service in the world. It's like America. We have a lot of problems, but very few of us want to trade our beautiful country for another.

The best way to stay out of trouble with the powers-that-be in the USPS -- the postal inspectors and such -- is to ship your orders when you should, take care of business as you should, give refunds if you say you will, and obey the laws as they pertain to all types of offers. Stay away from chain letters and similar garbage that can get you in trouble. Work closely with your local post office if you're doing bulk mail. They can show you ways to save a lot of money and they'll tell you exactly how they want to receive the mail so they can get it out quickly. Do everything that you can to be a good customer and they're going to treat you much better. Even better, establish a close relationship with a mailing house that works with the Post Office, so you don't have to.

One thing I want to add before I go on to our 25th and final secret is this: If somebody calls your shop and tells you they didn't receive their package, you need to ship them another one -- immediately. You need to make sure your customers have that order in their hands no matter what. You can usually depend on companies like UPS and Federal Express to get their packages where they're supposed to go, but with the postal service, we've found that a small percent of packages get lost on a regular basis. Often those packages are sitting somewhere else, unclaimed. So, that's one thing you have to be very cautious of: make sure you always ship them a new one if it's lost in the mail.

Now, on to our last tip, **Secret Number Twenty-Five**: just remember that all this gets easy after a while. The reason I listed this one last one is because sometimes, I think, people are overwhelmed when they hear all these ideas. The truth is that in and of itself, there can be an awful lot of things to learn about direct mail. But eventually you start to internalize them and it gets easier -- in fact, it can become a fun, challenging way to make money. Sure, it sounds complex at first. You think, "My goodness, I have to learn 101 things." But that's okay -- just learn them at your own speed. Eventually things just fall into line. It's so exciting and it can be so profitable. It offers a wonderful way to enjoy financial freedom and control over your life.

As your confidence grows, so will your income.

Knowledge is a great way to beat your fear. That's what this field is all about -- learning everything you can.